Common Enemy

Poems

Compiled and Edited by

Brian Sitta Kargbo

Sierra Leonean Writers Series

Common Enemy

Copyright © 2016 by Brian Sitta Kargbo (ed.)
All rights reserved.

ISBN: 978-99910-54-60-5

Sierra Leonean Writers Series

Table of Contents

Foreword	*iii*
Acknowledgments	*iv*
Dedication	*vi*
A Review – Oumar Farouk Sesay	*vii*
POEMS	
Paranormal Insinuation	1
Africa: My Mother Said	2
Pain	4
Time	5
Dark Days	6
Where Am I Going?	8
Chickens In Poultry	10
I'm A Winner	13
Bunch Of Roses	14
Game Lane	15
Stingy-Generousity	16
If Love	17
School Boys	19
Sweet Mama Salone	20
This Is Our War!	21
I Will Kill A Lion	22
The Shadow That Steals	25
A Kid's Story	26
Happy Funeral	27
Lamentation	29
A Day In School	30
The Shepherd	31
Rear Gem	32
A Cry For Freedom	33
Rain	34

Wake Up Brian!	35
Gloomy Picture	36
Plea	37
Unconventional Hero	38
The Seer's Mind	40
Veritas	42
Missing Times	47
Dark Memories	48
Power	50
Death	51
Life's Song	52
Modest Damsel	53
Save The Future	54
Confused	55
My Bad	56
The Beauty Of A Smile	58
The Person (An Identity Call)	59
A True Light	61
Future Fog	62
Rage	64
Warning	66
Rain And The Hen	67
Beastly Travesty {THE VOICE OF AN ANGRY BLACK AFRICAN}	68
Roadside	69
Voice Of The Village	70

FOREWORD

For far too long Sierra Leoneans have been reading and sitting to examinations on books authored by other nationals (for example Ghanaians and Nigerians). This anthology of poems has therefore been compiled to add to the growing body of literature by Sierra Leoneans and to encourage Sierra Leoneans to read works of their compatriots.

The poems were carefully chosen to have a relationship with the title of the anthology, *COMMON ENEMY*. The poets have looked at different issues that are "common enemies" or solutions to a sustainable progress in human life. Together, the poems will help the reader appreciate the steps to a positive living which get rid of the "common enemies" in our confused lives.

Brian Sitta Kargbo
Editor

ACKNOWLEDGMENTS

My first responsibility is to thank God Almighty (Ever living, ever faithful) for life, blessings and knowledge required in pursuing this task to completion.

I would ever remain indebted to members of my family (especially to people like Mr. Mohamed Conteh and my aunt Miss Marian I Sesay) for supporting me right through the venture of putting together an anthology. I particularly want to thank my mother for being there for me at all times. She deserves to be esteemed.

I am grateful to my "Best friend", Ayesha Munu, for her love and concern. I appreciate her support during the preparation of this book, especially her late night calls, typing the manuscript, assistance in editing the poems and sharing her creative ideas throughout the production of this book. Her interests were genuine and I wouldn't have completed this book without her guidance. I say thanks to her.

I would also want to thank the contributing poets. I appreciate their trust in contributing to the book. Reaching the 50 poems mark was really Herculean. May God richly bless them.

I finally would want to thank all those who gave me a hand and pieces of advice in the editing of the poems, reviewing the book and in one way or the other inspiring me. These include my pastor, Pastor Pette-Dalton of Wesleyan Church Brookfields, friends like Daniel Sillah (Spider Man), Samuel Hassan Turay, Elhaj Mohamed Sallieu Barrie, Bobson Rahman Kargbo Jr. Victor Mambu, members of the Sierra Leone Broadcasting Cooperation Voice Of Children (VOC) and the Activists on Point Team,

Mr.Joe Abass Bangura, and Madam Anita Koroma. I especially want to thank my mentor, Dr Gbanabom Hallowell for offering to read and correct the final manuscript; Professor Osman Sankoh (Mallam O) and the rest of the selfless team at Sierra Leonean Writers Series (SLWS) for giving me and the young contributors to this anthology an opportunity to show the world what we are made of; Salone Writers Forum (whatsapp) members for their criticisms and recommendations; Mrs Christiana Archibald, the Munu Family and a long list of God's children. Thank you all.

DEDICATION

This book is dedicated to my best friend, Ayesha...
we did it!

A Review

Brian Sitta Kargbo's edited anthology, Common Enemy, presents poems from young Sierra Leonean poets, freshly harvested by fresh minds and smelling like newly harvested crops. The alluring smell and freshness of the images appeal to the senses and tease the appetite of the reader. This collection signals a dawn in the literary landscape of Sierra Leone.

The themes of the anthology are many and diverse: identity, love, hate, nature and nostalgia. What is outstanding is the new perspective and images the young writers bring to these recurring themes in African literature. Whether the poet is "lost in the wind like an old promise" as in the poem; "where am I going"; or musing about childhood memories as in the poem, "A day in School," a vibrancy never before seen in a new generation of writers pulsates in every line.

These young writers survived childhood in a postwar Sierra Leone; born at the crossroads of a culture at a time when globalization and technology have flattened a once round world. The poets write at a time of new challenges, new identities on a continent that is still limping into the future; shackled by the burden of memories of a scarred past. Line after line these new realities are captured and laid bare on the page for the reader to make sense of a new age through their eyes.

In the poem "Reincarnation" we see the poet journeying from within in search of love, holding on to the image of a love that is worth waiting for even though the lover is just in the poet's imagination. Allusion drawn from the bible, the classics and the mundane points to an agile mind at work:

'I am Samson after the hair cut
I am Achilles minus the both heels'
The dexterity with which the poet moves from the classics
to the ordinary leaves the reader in awe:

'Loving you will pay
For my failed romance

When you frown I'll see smiles
So bright, the sun needs dark shades'

The poet's determination to wait for the true love of his life
that will make his heart pounds and hair tingles is anchored
on these last lines:

'We'll build bridges
Climb into each other's hearts
And never leave; no matter the hassle

But, it may not happen
I might stay this way
The forty years old bachelor
Haters might call me gay

But I'd rather be called gay
than connect without magic

Yes! I have other options
But I choose being hopeful, that one day...

Rose will run past me
Ooh boy! Trust me, the rest will be history!'

In "Chicken in Poultry," the poet deploys prose poetry to capture the helplessness of the hoi polloi in a political game that plays them like pawns in a chess board.

'We have been living in this city, rolling from one problem to another yet we claim to be in unity. Our vulnerability they use as a campaign for prosperity. We labour for the crafty, mentality so filthy with pity, and still wondering why we cannot own a building so lofty and with quality in our city. Oooh... What a pity.'

Some poems deal with themes of determination to succeed against all odds, others deal with the themes of African struggle, drawing strength from giants of African struggle like Nelson Mandela and others are just nostalgic poems capturing school days with playful yet effective imagery.

"Happy Funeral" is among the many poems that treat the recurring theme of corruption which runs throughout the collection. Witness these lines:

'They dance gleefully in riches, assumed through corruption and fetish. Our lives are wretched and brutish, but they swim in wealth like fishes, Ohh... this is rubbish —we were so foolish to surrender our desires and positive wishes, and though we yawn, four times a day they keep selecting dishes.

My heart bleeds with anger like a raging storm; as I ponder: "when will our time come?" But, it's a daily norm as they keep fooling us in this humdrum.'

It is obvious that the fifty poems in this Anthology written by young poets edited by a younger poet will fill a yawning gap that has mocked the country's literary scene for years. Like all literary works there are pitfalls in the collections like in cases where clichés are elevated to the profound and in few cases the end rhymes consume authenticity of the poems.

On the whole this Anthology will ever be remembered for what it has achieved; connecting our literary past and the present into the future.

Oumar Farouk Sesay
Author of
The Edge of a Cry (a collection of poems) – SLWS, 2015
Landscape of Memories (a novel) – SLWS, 2015

POEMS

PARANORMAL INSINUATION

Brian Sitta Kargbo

Conscience is divine
It runs through my spine
I can't decline
What's mine...

Success is designed
Happiness assigned
Progress is combined
With love aligned

My power I find
The Devil I bind
God's love is kind
Heaven in my mind

My mind is my alter
Greatness I'm after
Dues is my master
Equanimity potter

My man like the maker
Manna's baker
Original; no faker
A genius laker

My paranormal insinuation
An occidental confession
A coincidental obsession
A monumental confection

1

AFRICA: MY MOTHER SAID

Brian Sitta Kargbo

The old Africa is pregnant,
By night stories;
By a hot history; lingering;
By the blood of her children
Spilled dip in her.

Our ebullient Africa is now weak,
By the aspirations of her young;
The signs of hope in her protruding breast;
Of her kindred,
Sleeping in the earth with skulls and no brains;
Some with native skulls and foreign brains;
And those with brains of little senses.

Our beautiful Africa is pregnant for the world.

A new Africa will be born;
A son.

The new Africa will be a man!
A strong man!
Leading to greatness!
Loved by all!
The people's Africa!

Bearing a name dug out from hardship!
Stained with innocent sacrificial blood!
Into the kiln in Namibia!
From the tunnels of Ethiopia!
Bold like the name of Sankara!
Unshaken like Mugabe!
Shinning like gold from Ghana!

Revered like Mandela!
A powerful name; AFRICA!

This son will amaze the Asians!
He will be honoured in Australia!
Sought and reverenced by the Americans!
And followed by Europeans!

He will be half richer
Than the home in the sky.

gods of citadels!
The idols of government!
Criminals and honest men!
All coloured people!
Wherever they may be!
Will bow to him!

We await you Africa;
Come and take your place.
Africa, come forth!

PAIN

Umu Sall

Is it a game or what?
But my name and a game lane are not the same
Oh I have suffered in your hot paws!
Thanks for helping me out even when you hurt me
Why me? Oh pain why?
But once there's life, there's definitely hope

Pain comes your way to destroy your aim
You'll be in shame, 'cause pain takes away your fame
And name, to the drains
But be steadfast and focused
How firm you stand is what makes you gain

You have no friend; you're heartless
You are a bane and a demon
You make us speechless and faithless
Pain brings sadness, madness, and carelessness in our works

But I say, keep your hopes up
There'll be no room for pain
It will briskly run as if chased with a cane
And your dreams will surely reign

TIME

Tamba Temoindor Ngegba

Time turns the weather hot and cold, which makes you grow old
Time is something you can't buy and keeps ticking even after you
die
Always respect time
You can't break time— it helps you learn from mistakes
Time doesn't grant your wishes; use it wisely, it will bring you
riches
With the blink of an eye time passes by; handle every second
soberly
Time is limited. We always want more but never will
Time has no end; the realization of its significance makes you
better
Time makes you choose between wrong or right and vice versa
Time is something you could regret, if you behave like a
serpent
Time is a treasure that leads you to either good or bad
pleasure when a choice is made
Time is never enough
Always respect time. The disrespect of time makes you lose
respect for the future.
Always use TIME wisely!

DARK DAYS

Brian Sitta Kargbo

Within the memories of living men
of my beloved nation
Ebola is incomparable.
It sacrificed the souls of my people
On the altar of "don't touch!"
It rocked Mama Salone's head;
Its eyes became weary with constant mourning;
Salone's future was bleak;
Its thoughts were narrow.

Why was it so vile and ignorant of life?
That it fall our hands on our heads heavily?
Cowed us with ruthless laws!
How nauseating!

Ooh Ebola do not come back!
For we will kill you!
And bury your body in the land of never return!
Blind your eyes!
Cripple your stupid legs!
Broke your every limb!
Cage your soul in rear conscience!
And give you a heart with unmatched sorrow!
Reminding you of your every deed till you die a second death!

If your ears were pierced
With the screams and shrieks of the wounded and dying
Maybe, you wouldn't have been so anxious to attack either

But since you played oblivious!
Since you shamed us!

Made ambulances to almost deafen us!
Made 117 a part of us!
You made nations afraid of us!
Disrespected us!
Bruised us!
Killed us!
For three days you sat us!

Ebola, you will pay!
Yes! We have defeated you
But you'll pay someday

You stirred our ire with the loss you caused
I tell you
It will rankle across the decades
And endured until the death of our last generation

That pain you too will die from!
No nurse will care for you!
No doctor will save you!
The children will not play with you!
Even the undertakers will throw you!
And no god will forgive you!

Alone you'll go!
Alone you'll suffer!
Every nation will reject you!
You will be missed by your beneficiaries
But Hades will welcome you

WHERE AM I GOING?

Jesse Cobna-Davies

Just a lonely boy in this great world,
Finding a place to fit in
Lost in the winds like an old promise
I look like a bird lost from its nest
Lost because I seek answers and want a bite from the world's
wisdom cake
But, i'm scared of this world
It's bigger and crooked than I expected.
I'm confused!
My parents' spoken words I remember
And I ask myself: "where am I going?"

I left home without a clue
Left without thinking of what life holds for me
Left like an unarmed soldier pursuing an enemy

In my head I hear the voice of my mama calling…
Dad's voice too; telling her not to worry

Now i'm far from home, and I am lost
Even my shadow is lost from me…
Sitting in the dark I wonder and think about what's up in the
sky— the dark blue sky
I whisper to myself
"It is true, I am lost and I don't know where I am going"

I sit in the church and hear the pastor preach
His message heals and my heart is touched
My soul jump in affirmation as I open my mind for his words to
flow

'Cause even though i'm slow
I don't want my life to end in HELL so low
He spoke about Eternity— life after death
And he asked: "Where are you going?"

"My boy! My boy!
Your lies lead you out here;" he said
"Your sins weigh you down;
You're just like a balloon lost in the wind
But your true self lies in your mind
Find yourself at all cost!
Bring yourself back and it's a must! " He advised.
But I thought aloud
"Where do I go from here?"

CHICKENS IN POULTRY

Brian Sitta Kargbo

We have been living in this city, rolling from one problem to another yet we claim to be in unity. Our vulnerability they use as a campaign for prosperity. We labour for the crafty, mentality so filthy with pity, and still wondering why we cannot own a building so lofty and with quality in our city. Oooh... What a pity.

We are not considered a priority in this country. Our locality is plunged with poverty; no proper sanity, poor electricity and educational facilities; low food availability, low agricultural productivity; lack of parental responsibility; unanswered cases of teenage pregnancy with high infant mortality. The mind of school-going children is dirty with shopping, sex, "chilling" and party. What is the destiny of this country?

Instead of affability to fellow citizens, it is harsh hospitality with an affinity to people from overseas. No friendship, it is lesbianism and homosexuality. Our posterity is doomed for uncertainty in this **revengeful country**.
The streets are so filthy, gruesome accidents with uncountable fatalities. Political party plurality with the mentality to drain our "most talked about economy," creating tribal dichotomy, negatively influencing youthful debauchery with high alcoholic availability, for a second think it's honey, and ends in brutality geared by self– purchased stupidity.

"Politricks" with its sycophancy, verbosity, rivalry, its promise for a developed society with better facilities, all these ingenuities has dragged our once witty mentality to be naughty and parochially myopic making us unable to see beyond our communities and realizing our God-given qualities.

Politicians and their treachery is no more history but a reality. The state of the masses is celebrated as a national festivity.

Pastors, we expect to be holy, but, their message of vanity jeopardizes the possibility for eternity. Mohammedans with their mystery and harem of wives plausibility and roaming recitation clarity are just a show of fanatic spirituality.

Musicians and their parody to an international celebrity sways the senses of their gullible pig-headed followers to accept whole heartedly beastly realities preached at their warlike and feared rallies, deliberately swinging us from the messages we yearn for truly. What a sorrow to live in captivity.

The media clams to avoid a parley by concealing vital information from us, creating a cemetery platform making our lives risky and open to all forms of negativity amidst colour diversity which infringes on our developmental celerity which should enable us to live a life so worthy.

Universities are now training grounds for un-patriotic tendencies and immoral activities with the desire to join the tarantella of office holders who fulfill the prophecy with an intensity to turn our lives into **CHICKENS IN POULTRY.**

Our foreign policy objective greets us from the air and warmly welcomed with folly under the **SELF-AGGRANDIZEMENT THEORY** by pundits in making poverty our national destiny.

Our lives are complicated. No jobs– were aggravated. Negativity is perpetrated, we fight but we're persecuted. Look at us - the masses is malcontented; our thin hopes are dislocated, when will we be integrated? Borrowed lives we live, everything is imitated. Vague economic growth; we're easily intoxicated.

It is only when we realize, that there is a need to harmonize, we

11

can never stop living our impermanent lives in disguise. We labour for a grain of rice, dinning hungrily with flies, and still cannot actualize the status in our mind's eyes.

They steal our franchise with lies to enrich their lives, with all our cries, they still pretend not to recognize, with artificial myopia, and rise and slice our victimized ties with hypocritical and corrupt knives with an intention to demoralize and dichotomies our unstable lives. With honey lips they spit ice into our fickle minds, knowing our desire to organize and destabilize their vicious devices, aimed at sharply reducing our unalienable human price.

THIS IS FOR THE "FOOLISH," I'M CALLING THEM TO BE WISE.

I'M A WINNER

Brian Sitta Kargbo

I am walking on the dusty path to reach my desired goal
My feet are dirtied by the mountain of brown flour in the Sahara
Desert
Running to the Province of Freedom I heard Nelson Mandela's
cry from Soweto
I perspire as I climb the Kilimanjaro to overlook Abba Father's
majesty
Thirst for fresh water, I bend to drink from the Nile River
 I'm pierced with a bullet from Somalia.

My patriotic zest is geared by Nehemiah's boldness
I see my chariot of fire; my debonair good deeds are rewarded
Forgiveness is my motto, my betrayers are free
I am Moses! I am Moses! I will lead my people
Joseph mentored me to patiently wait for my destined time
Samballat and Tobias from me they run,
Solomon is my name –to be great I was born
Who am I to be chosen? I ask my Mosaic conscience
I am close to the heart of God, so I dance with glee at his
majesty

Please tell Obama I'm coming, gliding with Michael Jackson's
feet
My riches are plenty so Jesse James chase after me
But I swing blissfully on Rastafari Makonen's dread with Bai
Bureh's heart

The world is a stage; i'm part of the cast
With obedience as the watch word, prosperity comes faster
THANK GOD ALMIGHTY
I'M A WINNER!

BUNCH OF ROSES

Brian Sitta Kargbo

Love is a natural phenomenon
Together with your love one should be a norm
Immaculate it is, love cannot be hidden
Cold or hot, it has no season

Popularly known but it couldn't be seen
All carry it- in the heart it's in
We need it in our lives, even the stubborn
For I experienced it just when I was born

Brings peace to lives when it's present
The oppressed need it give them as present
Demonstrated by all, even THE MOST HIGH
To kill it, the evil one will try

GAME LANE

Haja Isatu Bah

Whenever I think of corruption I go insane
With a heavy heart and a confused mind, I bear the pain
The innocent thieves have destroyed my nation; when shall it
rain?
My beloved nation, when shall things become new again?

The name corruption sweeps us to the dark away from the light
Slowly my happiness is fading, how can my future be bright?
I have a lot to say my mind is in fright
I wish I were the leader; I would have taken my nation to the
greatest height

The walls of hope built with staggering unity have almost
crumbled
My joy and laughter has metamorphosed themselves to
trouble
No honest leaders to care for us and lead us out of this jungle
Money and fame is all they want; why can't they be humble?

I wish I were the leader to take my people to the right path
I would love and care for them from the auricles and
ventricles of my heart
Corruption! I curse you to be minimized in planet Earth!
And let us live happily and put the horse before the cart

STINGY-GENEROUSITY

Brian Sitta Kargbo

It's good, they say; to be a leader
But woe, to be a looser
Splendour, affluence and influence you enjoy
At the top of affairs is an unmatched joy

Corruption and strife you promised to deviate
But all we could feel is destitution and hate
Hostility and affray you said we won't see
Tracks on our faces, is this how it should be?

Clandestine activities, all we see is darkness
The land is suffering, and yet you're careless
To your promises of HEAVEN you're now perfidious
Your wicked-affability is just too obvious

The tarantella of your ambiguous activities is detestable
We could lynch you scoundrels, and could be imperceptible

IF LOVE

Brian Sitta Kargbo

If love had eyes
It would have seen Cupid's arrow:
The anguish of dogmatic lovers,
The foolishness of craving,
The lust in mortals,
Love should have seen deceit...

If love could talk
It would have denied 'fakers':
It would tell us who cares and who doesn't,
Maybe it would have told us who first betrayed it and
Who defiles it chastity,
Why it suffers me...
By now, it would have answered all our questions.

If love had ears
It would have quickly suffered deafness
From the issues of sinners
Who pests it with fairy tales...

If love had arms
It would embrace all mankind:
All races, ages and faces from varying places.

If love had a heart
It would have meant its love:
It would have loved,
Or maybe, it would have been biased,

Love would have understood our plights,
It would have been conscious of stress.
If love had a heart it would have saved me from the very many

17

deaths I've died,
It would have sacrificed its soul for me,
It would have accentuated virtual peace.

If love could understand
My pain,
My groans,
The unfortunate riot in my head,
The turbulence in my loins.

Love is bombastic but not realistic,
Promising, but not all encompassing,
Supercilious of hate
But, oblivious of fate.

SCHOOL BOYS

Brian Sitta Kargbo

School boys now tend to be bad,
Playing pranks on girls and making them sad.
"I love you," "I miss you;" those are what they say
But they just want to get you, for an hour or day.

They may be gentle, sweet and charming
But lust for their honey lips will leave you crying.
By their looks, they're handsome, neat and cool
But don't give in! Be careful!

Although some girls are just like them,
With different kinds of lovers like books to a pen.
Their 'modus-operandi' they regard as necessary,
To have erotic partners they see as lovely.

As school going children, learn to love your books!
Don't be keen on lovers, they may be crooks!
ABC, 123, those are what you should know,
Don't follow those cunning mortals; it's your boat they'll row!

SWEET MAMA SALONE

Alfred Dravie Parry

Sweet Mama Salone
Filled with magnificent grace
A land endowed with natural resources
Blessed with a peaceful atmosphere

Sweet Mama Salone
We pledge our devotion, our strengths and our mights
We pray that no harm on thy children may fall
Great is the love we have for thee

Sweet Mama Salone
Your knowledge and truth our forefathers spread
Ever we seek to honor thy name
So may we serve thee ever alone

Sweet mama Salone
We show forth the good that is ever in thee
Defend your children, and give them wisdom
Strengthen us with grace and unite us in peace

THIS IS OUR WAR!

Brian Sitta Kargbo

Trekking miles to motherhood,
In persistent dragging attitude,
Weariness details her unbreakable skin
But her haughtiness and difference make her faith spin

In a system plagued with mortality
She portrays sanity.
"On this bed kings are born,
On this bed queens have gone,
On this bed I must survive;"
She mumbles

Like a leaky unstaunched wench,
Fragmented thoughts of victory cloud her mind.

Disconnecting herself from the irregularities
She dreams of her child;
Her President; her future.
She must hand with health illuminates,
Rotten facilities should not intimidate.

Safe motherhood breeds better livelihood.

As if welcomed to feast,
Her foetus beams and kicks obliviously;
Totally unaware of its battles.
It makes an obdurate victory
Into evil,

Into the hands of naive Nightingale,
Into a worry world.

After greeted with affection,
Children have wept.
After yelling with passion,
Some gems have slept.
Through the paws of poor services,
To the jaws of fake promises,
The child and its mother die
The land and its men guise

It is our war, let's fight it!

I WILL KILL A LION

Brian Sitta Kargbo

Today, I will kill a lion
Whether big or small;
I will kill a lion.

I'm ready for its paws;
Sharper than knife,
Or its deadly teeth,
Capable of tearing stone,
Or its face,
That drives men to their early doom.

Many times have I scared death
Even pain denies me.
A lion's roar mustn't shake me.

Today, I will kill a lion.

I will light a fire,
Sing sweet songs,
Face a lion, and kill it.

Haunted by this lion
In a hungry attack,
In red robes,
With death sitting on its face,
At the apex of my youth,
As a prey in its eyes.

But, I must kill this lion.
Not as Samson,
Nor as Hercules,
But as a crippling child,

Sunk in naivety,

I touch its head,
Feel the roughness of its fur,
Hold its neck and slice it.

I said I would kill a lion;
The lion is dead.
Today I killed a lion.

THE SHADOW THAT STEALS

Brian Sitta Kargbo

I am the shadow that steals.
I usually come the time you wouldn't expect.
Many people don't like me;
Neither to talk about my name, 'cause they hate me.

From the beginning of life I was around;
When Adam and Eve were driven my name was sounded.
I take the lives of people and make their relatives cry.
And, I'm here forever; I will never die!

Sometimes I feel pity and want to cry,
For those who wonder and ask me "why?"
For taking the lives of the faithful,
And leaving the wicked ones to roam idly.

Anyway, I'm just doing my job.
I bring you down when you're at the hub.
Some people love life so much and want to live forever,
They don't want to die and be covered

Sometimes, people pray against me,
Just to push me away because they hate me.
People call me "THE DESTROYER OF DREAMS"
For I wash them away, so they say i'm mean

If I say much you'll be annoyed
You'll say I'm wicked –I don't make you enjoy
Goodbye my friends! But listen: I want you to love me
I'm only a mere servant, so you see…

A KID'S STORY

Brian Sitta Kargbo

Let's dance in the rain,
Let's dance out our pain.
The rain is our brother;
He makes all things fun.
Even as we wonder,
We wrestle and we run.

Old people are jealous,
They cannot be like us.

The rain has a drumbeat,
Those only children hear.
He tells us a secret,
One we take so dear.

We keep waiting for the rain,
We want to jump out again.

Rain, can you come every day?
We children want to play.

HAPPY FUNERAL

Ishmael Nyallay

Dead dreams, bad days, we're disillusioned with folded arms and feet as gold tears drop from our eyes. We're getting old, goods have been sold, falsehood is been told, we yearned for better days but these couldn't hold. It seems like we were just too bold for the future that we joyfully sold.

They dance gleefully in riches, assumed through corruption and fetish. Our lives are wretched and brutish, but they swim in wealth like fishes, Ohh... this is rubbish —we were so foolish to surrender our desires and positive wishes, and though we yawn, four times a day they keep selecting dishes.

My heart bleed with anger like a raging storm; as I ponder: "when will our time come?" But, it's a daily norm as they keep fooling us in this humdrum.

But it seems as though our lamentations have become a catalyst for yelp from the privileged few with a thoughtful consultation. But, it's like they have become unpleasant with their ecstatic acts in their rejection concert because everyone has slowly become violently disobedient to their cozy life of popinjay.

Their diabolical hysteria has created this unanimous ethos as we revolutionary make pain-joy headway with artificial cockiness and sharpness.

Their time is at hand so they urge for a grand re-union in order for them to remain as our rich and privileged centurion.

They have become captives in their minds waiting to be rescued as they thought aloud: "we were in an air–filled catacomb but we never knew, and yet we guised as the rich and privileged few?"

27

This is a funeral, but we are happy.

We are sympathizing with them in peace, and it's time they know that.

LAMENTATION

Brian Sitta Kargbo

Oh God death is difficult!
You be part and don't exit, just like a cult.
When you're called you can't say "NO!"
You may be freed later, a time you don't know.

I came with joy and no clothes on,
But I left wearing something, and people who mourn.
The end of every man's life is death.
It cares less; healthy or wealthy.

Death is a thing none will miss;
You play your part and leave; that's the way it is.
If you die now we'll meet someday.
I'm left to think, rise or lay?

A DAY IN SCHOOL

Brian Sitta Kargbo

A day in school looks new and sweet.
When coming to it you look fresh and neat.
Teacher say, "sit down and be quiet!"
Above the law you go, severe thrashing you'll get.

Sometimes I reminisce my first day in school;
When I was young, childish and playful.
Tidy I come but untidy I'd leave;
In the school's compound I had always wanted to live.

A bag with school materials and water-bottle in my hand;
I moved along happily, by my leader's demand.
New friends I saw; young and old;
Boys and girls, whose destinies had unfolded.

We learn a lot when we are in school;
To rhymes and songs and our friends bull.
When school is over, we pray, and everyone goes home.
The thoughts go through my mind like hair in a comb.

THE SHEPHERD

Brian Sitta Kargbo

I know a man that is old and wise.
He reads the wind he reads the skies.
He knows when storms will blow his way.
He knows when rain will fall each day.

All day and night he tends his sheep;
He hears the bleating of his sheep.
There's not a lamb in his farm,
He hasn't carried in his arm.

I wish I knew the things he knows;
The night time skies, the wind that blows.
The singing birds, the bleating cries.
I wish I were a shepherd wise.

I wish I were to be like him;
The happiest man, that's how it would seem.

REAR GEM
(For my dear mum)

Brian Sitta Kargbo

My days are sad without my mummy.
I love her so much; she makes me happy.
You may be happy with daddy;
But for me, I love my mummy.

True love I felt, till I slept.
To napkins and pin, my butt was clipped
Sometimes I disturbed and cry all day;
Sweet songs she sang, and to the bed I was laid.

She knows when i'm hungry, worry or angry.
She tries to make me happy- to that, she hurries.
Even though I was naughty, troublesome and wild;
Yet, she taught me to be meek and mild.

She thrashed me, when I go wrong
I'll be annoyed with her but it wouldn't stay longer

I'm growing old but naughty; yet, she cares for me.
Who else could it be? Except my mummy.

A CRY FOR FREEDOM

Brian Sitta Kargbo

I'm a poor blind man.
My family is poor;
I have none to care for me...
My life is full of stress.

My filthy poor hands I stretch each day;
Expecting for the day.

No wife and children; i'm left alone.
With stressful days, my future is bleak.
With strife in my land, my destiny is toppled over.
Masters of portfolio –they're the nation's scoundrels.

I have no ruler;
I'm autonomous.

Tattered clothes like rags on my back,
I don't know what is keeping me alive.
They say my society is blessed, but, i'm sceptical.
Every day I think of who will be my JESUS;
To free me from the asperity of this world,
I CRY FOR FREEDOM!

RAIN

Brian Sitta Kargbo

It's noisy and cool, and makes the foliage wet.
Cool for drinking –it's the firmament's sweat.
Unprecedented it is, so none can bet.

Little drops so tender, it looks like tears.
Rude interruption, for none it fears.
Lure us to sleep, by the rhythm it bears.

WAKE UP BRIAN!
(For Brian Sitta Kargbo)

Marina J. Nyandebo

Brian, oh Brian!
The world is calling you.
Wake up! Wake up!
There is work for you to do.

Others are taking away your wealth,
While you are still in your slumber.
Get up now!
Or poverty will grip you!

Stop the illusion!
Brian you are free.
Take advantage of that freedom now!
You can be the greatest!

You must get up and work for yourself!
Stop begging from those strangers!
The pinnacle could be steep,
But, you can reach it today.

Teach your children to be industrious!
Teach them patriotism!
They will lead after you!

You are powerful!
Brian, let the world see it!

GLOOMY PICTURE

Brian Sitta Kargbo

Sitting in the hall with my pen unmovable,
Only concerned about words, and not imaginary
Numbers.
My heart sheer away from Maths; it isn't edible.
I can only answer to, "Who are the Boers?"

Thinking about poetry, it seems i've lost focus,
Mathematical terms seem to me as viruses.
Offering mathematics is really not my choice
"You should know maths!" I often hear this voice.

Escaping from classes 'cause we hate mathematics.
Not important to my future, the artist's mind clicks.
For History or Government, we are anxiously yearning;
All because Mathematics is a catalyst for sleeping.

We wish it could be an optional subject;
Ohh...we would hysterically say "**FREE AT LAST**!"
Many wish for this too, but it's only a dream;
So difficult and gloomy for many it seems.

PLEA

Brian Sitta Kargbo

The trumpet of truth is neglected to be covered with mud.
It's pathetic, we do not fear God.
We are trading our conscience –an essential life cord.
The WAR has begun; the fulfillment of the word.

In agony and destitution your people are molested.
The best men are VORACIOUS in the nation you're
Interested.
In our success we forget you, to our dexterity it's attributed.
Free us from captivity- to you we're indebted.

We live in INFIDELITY, even when we know.
What an unforgiving heart; we refuse to let go.
We will surely reap what we consciously sow.
For because we deny you, the world is in woe.

Clutched in poultry like a restricted hen.
THE COMING IS NEAR, but they still ask "when?"
Heading for doom, led by supposedly best men.
In grave danger and trouble: Daniel in the Lion's Den.

We are swift to sin with no hesitation;
Somber days, we need a TRUE CONFESSION.
The son brought life, and eternal connection.
Father, save us, or HELL will be our location!

Forgive us OUR SINS before the trumpet blows!
Guide us in your paths; save us from our foes!

UNCONVENTIONAL HERO
Dedicated to Casanova
Notorious womanizer and Italian Adventurer

Brian Sitta Kargbo

Handsome beyond words,
Yet ruled by lust for women;
You conquered them like fragile.
Kingdoms leaving a reign of ruins in your trail.
You, a harbinger of doom,
Whose gloom eclipse in their lives.

Where are you now?
Rotting in pieces!

No human being is immortal;
Now your mortality has got up with you.
Where are you now?
A mere mortal decaying!

Sly and cunning you were!
You guised yourself as an adventurer and threw sober men in
grief.
Oh you, you attacked every beauty!
They couldn't forestall your deceitful advances,
As your "smooth-leggedness" danced their hunch out.
Ludicrous! You played oblivious of conscience.

Charming in your tuxedo, you enchant with lust,
To sweat your bedding and put out your fire;
You did with wild emotions, words cannot mention.
Casanova, you were a daft but you never knew!
None is; I doubt if one will ever be,
You. The oddity who thought he was happy.

No more under the sun,
Where are you now? Casanova!

THE SEER'S MIND

Brian Sitta Kargbo

I [WHAT WAS]

There was a time when people sat still,
Now it's uproar; we want a doctor to heal.
There was a time when people do not kill;
Now we hate each other- we're wicked and can't feel.
There was a time when people do not 'chill,'
It's the order of the day now, by the elder and lil.
There was a time when people paid the bill,
Now we're corrupt in open air –we steal for a meal.
There was a time when people had no skill peel;
Now they believe, to be eye –catching, this is one seal.

II [WHAT IS]

Now people don't care;
Just do as you like; Judgment will pay the years.
Instead of God, we say work hard,
Destiny is a fable –we succeed by our card.
Now, we neglect peace,
We forgo sound doctrine and wish for a kiss.
Now the PRINCE OF HELL rules,
He tries to get many, by using his ghouls.
Now is the time when people say, "Let's go!"
But they still wish you fail and fall in woe.

III

In this time the Father we don't fear,
We try to hide, forgetting he's everywhere.
These days, there's less water, more beer;

For thy stomach sake, drink, forget about the seer.
These days any clothes we wear,
Women walk half naked, seductively looking for a peer.
In this time we do anything for the dough;
Independence is the best; a 'G' needs no co.
In this time we can't even hold a hoe;
These days' goodies hardly show;
These days everything is just worse;
Instead of blessings, it's like we're yearning for curses.
In this time we denounce God's gift;
Artificial we crave for, calling it a face lift.

IV [WHAT WILL BE]

There'll be a time when the world will unite;
We'd all be in harmony, and no need to fight.
There'll be a time we needn't fear snake bites.
There'll be a time we needn't worry to fly kites;
What's the essence? We'd already be in the height.
There'll be a time we would all be glowing in light;
The life of mankind would be shut: there'll never be a night.

Babylon will fall some day.
Yes! It surely will fall, I'm telling you; some day.
There'll come a time there'll be no hater,
So get ready for the master, forget about the paper.

One day angels will sing me sweet songs.
If you don't work for this, with the wicked you'll be among.

Smoking is dangerous, it affects your lungs.
There'll come a time we'll be punished for our wrongs.
Books will be opened; our deeds would be exposed;
We've get one last chance to do what we're supposed.
Remember, no one knows the day,
So go down on your knees and pray.

VERITAS

Brian Sitta Kargbo

I'm foolish; I need wisdom.
Many years i've prayed - when will my time come?
He is seated at the right hand; the virgin mother's son.
Why should we resolve problems through the barrel of a gun?
On the tree of trespass, He said "it is done;"
Jesus is the Christ; God is one.

The present was recorded in the past as a lesson for the future;
This is the biblical hour, we need to recapture.
The future is bright but we've lost our culture.
Catholic or Anglican is just an earthly signature.
Eternity is costly; it has its own expenditure.
The devil rules? I can't tell but conjecture.

Die and be judged or wait for his coming?
Stand up for something; give in not to everything.
Coup d'état, mass protests –we hear of suicide bombing.
If the streets were golden we would have dug up everything.
Why? You forgive me but I keep sinning.
Corrupt heads stay fresh and relaxed while dinning.

Which is? Heaven or Paradise?
It's a question for the scribes; they claim to be wise.
Hell will cry forgiveness, not for stealing, but for lies.
Oh... This world is doomed; when will we realize?

People will change, accept if they apologies
Every politician is a demon; they guise for our franchise.

We fight for what we know couldn't hold.
Shabbetai Tzevi's fire is cold.

Square up to the devil you need to be spiritually bold.
Warring times– bloody diamond and gold.
Israel has no face; his beloved son was sold
God knows best; someone once told.

The wicked succeeds and righteous perish.
Troubles and pestilences on the people you cherish.
White supremacy, black dolorous, and hypnosis.
He'll come when some punish and others flourish.
Does unity exist? Please tell me i'm foolish.
In this world if you aren't humane you're brutish.

I shed tears because I was told they heal.
Sickness has no holiday; it lurks to kill.
The faithfulness of Elshaddai is life's meal.
Judge justly adelphoi but climb truth's hill.
All songs are spiritual, they teach and heal.
I will sink the sea beneath the Earth- Yes I will!

The world is mystical but beings are cynical.
Getting I AM's attention is simple –lyrical.
What we do tell on us, the doctrine is practical.
Up and down, round and round; life is cyclical.
Make the change and be sure –social or political.
Freedom is a wish, the books says our lives would be critical.

What gives knowledge? God or books?
A passion for fashion, we're concerned about looks.
Life's not easy; I keep sending my old hook;
They can't wait to get theirs, by hook or by crook.
What a wonderful world; six days He took.
Buried carcasses, roaming souls, learn more from the
Egyptian book.

We must all die;
Some didn't, others wouldn't; but why?

It's the same thing that distinguishes us –you and I.
Life is sweet; if you love it, you die.
Let children be children, their home is in the sky.
Pretty faces end a war; have you ever asked "why?"

We have one destiny - Heaven or Hell.
Choice makes us humans so Macbeth fell.
Fear not; in the cell or in death's dell.
With a tunnel vision, all will end well.
Can I be rich if I sell?
If I'm hurt who should I tell?

Things and times change;
The more we know the faster we change.
It's funny how people change;
If he's mean, cast spell– leprosy or headaches…
I'm weak so forgive me if I make mistakes.
Sin is sweet so we take more like chocolates.

Withheld me from sinning against thee;
If I die today Lord please remember me.
My heart is deceitful; the prophet said you know me.

I don't know about you, but I know what would be;
At the third coming a New Jerusalem would be.
Take up your cross and follow me.

Oh God of the poor, why do you protect wicked leaders?
They silently broke the laws and pretend to be the healers.
I do not need a mascot when faith works wonders.
The world has lost its wealth, its children die of hunger.
To be a God is easy but there's one Jehovah.
Hate is necessary, it makes us greater.

Emerald, carbuncle, onyx and sapphire;
Those minerals for nature's beauty have always been here.
They made us from dust, angels from fire.
Spread your legs around, success is so rear.
Listen to truth; i'm convinced it knows where.
Peace will never exit so long as we are here.

Abba Father reigns forever, beings will always be subject.
A Heavenly action produces an earthly reaction with no
Regret.
A feudal world; we live to praise and give respect,
Dimidium facti qui coepit habet.
Pour down your divine blessings, Lord make us wet.
He made many beauties our agency alone cannot select.

My heart is weak; temptations are hard to handle;
I need your help or i'll fall with this bundle.
With flesh and blood, spirits too I wrestle.

It's better to be on his side –he's our shield in battle.
Don't get it twisted: prayer brings more trouble.
Cut the veins of my ego, help me to be humble.

God loves all His children to the last day;
The covenant is certain; Christ rose on the third day.
He prepares us for greatness, pain is one way.
Lo the fall of Babylon! No seer can tell the day.
Make hay during the day that you may get the pay.
For those who survive, there's always another day.

Can a mortal man be righteous before God?
No one can. He who is, is himself a God.
Exalted among men is an abomination to God.
Faust lusts for magical power so he made Lucifer his god.
A friend of the world is an enemy of God.
If demons are powerful, why do they fear God?

In these days can I marry without courtship?
I've got more and i'm tired of counting ship.
Their thoughts are erotic; they denounce two-sex friendship.
Who should we worship? Elshaddai or Your Lordship?
Between Lucifer and Mephistopheles is a strong relationship.
I'm the same person but I converse with sprits in my sleep.

Degrees don't make educated men —experience does.
Circumstances cannot limit God's work through us.
Every man is superstitious; we believe YESHUAH open doors.

In spite of courage disaster drains us.
We are all the same —positivity and negativity exist in us.
We are slaves to sin but not like Aesop or Spartacus.

Return the Kickapoo's their land for God's sake.
But, under what authority did you take?
Death is certain but happiness is a fake.
At our weakest points lips can cause earthquake.
Magic lives forever; the Magnen David was awake.
In his image he created us —for His pleasure's sake.

Some prayers for sure will never be answered.
Goals must be specific; some thoughts should be reserved.
To King Solomon's magical signet demons and sprits
Answered.
Nowadays, respect is not easily earned; you have to fight for it.

MISSING TIMES

Grace Bella-Kamara

It's noon; product of the fresh morning.
I'm still here, but not as you knew.
Old ways have changed but breathing continues.
Time flies; yes it does.

Years of toiling; some were gloomy, some joyful.
Somehow, I leant to be awake and alive.
I can't believe they're gone; I'm missing times.
Where the ugly were made beautiful and vice versa.

Some were hooked up in pedagogue snares for neglect of plain
truth.
We ignored but it paid off.
The best times but not the happiest- of course.
I am missing times.

Those friends and their grimace I miss.
Teachers, oh teachers I miss dearly.

Things change once there's growth and success.
It's an end and it sure.

It is God.
It is His favor;
It is His grace;
It is His strength to endure...
Ah! At last the mauve and white is off!!!

DARK MEMORIES

Emmanuel B. Conteh

Times go by like the water in River Mano.
The memories in my box are as the back of a tortoise.
I remember, yes I remember.
The giant cork crowing as we startle from wonderland into the
world of choice.

I remember the fresh and chilly dawns;
The passionate rivers and their reoccurring rhythms;
The birds as they whistle their favorite sweet songs;
Oh yes! I remember.
The memory of our last usual gatherings in the open dust field;
Where traditions and cultures were thrown at us by the god's
chosen.

I remember the obscurity of the incantations;
The numerous and witty parables of grey hairs;
Those days I remember, Oh those days…
The days of cultured luxury lingers in our gullible minds.

In hysteria we move our joints to the calling leather, in our
annual celebrations in this same dusty fields with the
wrinkled and fresh.
Unity, love and harmony were the languages we spoke.

I remember those who came in floating woods.
Strangers they were — claiming to have brought
the manual for growth.

And shame oh shame we held their knowledge and neglected our
taboos with careless abandon.
Those strangers untied our knot of brotherhood and placed a

sabre in our business.
Ingrates! Devils! Thieves!
All these they did by their dangerous dexterity!

We go red with rage each time we remember.
But what did we get? What have we got?
What are we getting?
Empty gloomy thoughts.
I remember.
My people remember.

POWER

Noel Wright

I do not crave to be in power;
Yet, I hate it not.
Power is like grains of sand,
It is lost easily when much is gathered.

Power is destruction.
The mind of man is weak to control it.
It is meant for serious and foresighted mortals with good hearts.
Though many try to get it at length,
Its blood stops where awareness grows.

I seek three powers from you dear God.
Give me the power to think;
Give me the power to stand by it;
With these I have the powers of the world.

DEATH

Ayesha Munu

Always around us;
Watching, waiting,
Waiting, watching.
As we go about our daily races.
Going nowhere;
Achieving nothing;
Thinking that we have it all,
And then it strikes.
When we least expect it,
It shows us that we're really not superiors.
No one can escape...
It takes it all.
Forever gone.
Yes, it helps us remember;
The memories remind us to take it easy.
Spend more time with family and friends,
Because you never know,
When you'll go.
Death,
Always around us;
Let it go.

LIFE'S SONG

Brian Sitta Kargbo

Love is business
Patience is speechless
Man is hopeless
Hope is breathless
Dreams are flawless
Failure is careless
God is guiltless
Thoughts are lawless
Age is meaningless
Death is fearless
Strength is shapeless
Success is crestless
Spirits are restless
Life is priceless
Beauty is tasteless
Nothingness is fruitless
Conflict is rootless...

MODEST DAMSEL

Mai Tumani Fonnie

Bounded in emotional bliss; she's a treasure rear.
There are many…but none as bright and sound.
Her eyes, her smile, her hands…
Yes, those smile again;
As fresh and genuine like the morning breeze.

Precious is her heart like sparkling gold;
A gift to behold;
Wise men and idiots, all tossing coins for her favor;
In the shadows I admire her;
In "somber" I taste her beauty.

Like Da'Vinci with his brush on a canvas;
She's a glowing piece of fine art — a priceless gem.

Evening light, clouded skies and chilly breeze,
The ceiling light sat on her soft cheeks.
A modest smile of affection was all she gave.
She was close, so close that I felt
The atmosphere was making a good impression on
Her facial expression.

A moment to souvenir;
Lots of words, but her as shy,
To look me in the eye
Maybe covered by the sensuality of word's blanket.
But, a shy look was all I got.
Her heart's song and smile worth it all.

SAVE THE FUTURE

Haja Mariama Kamara

We did not apply to be born,
Why do you consider us a burden?
You were born and cared for.
Make your tomorrow today;
Give us preference and care.

Resources are the fruit of life;
The best resource is human.
Your future depends on us.
Make your future today;
We need preference and care.

The future depends on us.
Who will be your future leaders?
Once a man; twice a child.
Make our future bright;
Give us preference and care.

What future do you have for us?
Where are our rights?
What foundation have you made?
What does the future hold for us?
Where is the preference and care?
We deserve better treatment as children.

CONFUSED

Brian Sitta Kargbo

If I die will you cry?
Please tell me why
So I can know what to buy
And, make its true; don't LIE
I used to think death's nigh
But life's sweeter then pie
As I sigh with wide eyes
MY TIE MAKES ME WISE

Passion is a fatigue to the heart
But, does dream know that?
Forgetting there's tomorrow makes me fat
In HONOUR I duff my hat
To the road of freedom shown on the mat
In silence, like the meekness of a cat
Death takes no bath
It says, because it treads on the same path...

MY BAD

Grace Bella-Kamara

It was not my plan...
Neither was it my dream…
The thought of my tomorrow was bright;
Going to school with high hopes;
But all seems to be shattered now.

Stop blaming me!
No one seemed to care:
Among my little siblings
I was forced to act like a "mama;"
With books as food and pen as water? No!
What do you think?

You should've advised me;
But you left me freely.
Though I recalled aphorisms from school,
I still wanted to have a feel of it….just once.
But now I am stocked.

Stop blaming me!
I never noticed the signs quickly…
Oh Teenage Pregnancy;
A victim I have now become.
I can't afford to hurt the baby;
Do I have a choice?

Oh my, Oh why?
I ought to have known better;
I misplaced what mattered most;
But I cannot blame myself…

Who then, if not me?
At least I should have stayed in school.

It is my fault!
Not my parents',
Neither the community,
Not on the school's heads,
Neither the society I live in.

I am the owner of my future.
I should've chosen the light.
But how come I didn't discern earlier?
Was I a pupil of lust?
Now the claws of apprehension grips me,
As I mourn my thoughtless choice.

I believe I will rise again,
And prove to the world that I am a potential.
But I was careless;
It's my bad.

THE BEAUTY OF A SMILE

Brian Sitta Kargbo

Smiles are deceptive.
Are grins receptive?
But smiles are helpful.
The catacomb is starved when muscles go
Cheerful.
Happiness is measured by the width of its smile;
Some for long; others for a while.

I live to smile.
I love to smile.
The world is my oyster.
Smile is my countenance booster.

Death is hesitant to a smiling face;
Smile is a lubricant to a conflict base.
Anguish besets where smile is bereft.
Forever young; smiles are forever young.

THE PERSON
(AN IDENTITY CALL)

Brian Sitta Kargbo

Who am I?
I'm from a godly race;
With my mama's grace;
With a ruler's face;
In conscience case;
With TRUTH'S pace.

Who am I?
I am the singing voice,
With the loudest noise;
I'm akin to boys,
With their dreaming toys;
Yes. I am that voice.

Who am I?
I am something.
Wanting everything...
Getting many things;
Doing many things;
Keeping one thing.

Who am I?
I'm a dust,
With no cost.
The last, but i'm first.
I'm just just;
I'm not the worst.

Who am I?
I am that strange mortal,
Basking in sincere moral;

With three lives...total.
Not a work of portal.
I am royal.
Valuable like riyal;
Originality; i'm real.

Who am I?
I am conscience's bell,
In identity cell.
I'm a well;
Sweet like mell;
Generous – I don't sell.
I can't tell;
But, all is well.

Who am I?
I am a king;
With white wings;
So sing...

Who am I?
I am precious.
Different from the previous...
I am righteous and serious.

A TRUE LIGHT
(For The Prince Of Wales School– Kingtom)

Brian Sitta Kargbo

From 1925,
Our hearts your glory dived.
Our bond is a rock; what mortal can rive?
Your success has never had five,
Your greatness is alive;
Your name will survive.

A Palace of nobility;
Envy to society;
White souls are never lazy as they call for prosperity;
A nation in a nation; simple obscurity.

I'm a PrinceWalean with quality.
When others fake it, PrinceWaleans show originality.
Sparkling semblance, with akin crafty ability.

Eloquence lives on;
Evidence from yon;
Consistency in con;
Immortality for eon.

FUTURE FOG

Brian Sitta Kargbo

My girlhood is not a mistake.
Why jeopardize my future
with culture sharp paranoia?

My sight is indistinct;
Heart distending from inner slagging;
It's like hopes are lost.
Daily I live in fear.
Is your action venial?
Such a barbaric trait!

I toast myself at excellence fire,
When methinks subjection?
My brother's face not different;
Why do I have to call for recognition?

I'm violated, derived and jeered at!
My home demeans me.

Is that the reward for being a girl?
Is that the nature of man?
Finding solace in a birdling?
Prising into my pride?
Uncovering my covering, violently?
That foolery has to stop!
It is not virility!

Girls can make a change;
Be mindful of the years.

Taste my thoughts;

Let the world taste my thoughts!

Allow us to use our comeliness and sassiness,
For the world's happiness.
Do not inflict us with fear;
It is our right to be here!

RAGE

Brian Sitta Kargbo

Bloody toes,
Red fingers,
White bedding turns red;
All bloody!!!

Day and night it lurks.
At a sight I prick;
Annoyingly I prick.
It scatters bloody stench,
Anywhere it chooses;
From bedding to clothes,
Clothes to the "pricker;"
Bloody wretch!!!

Hard to find.
At day it disappears, or lurks surreptitiously.

So I reach for a spray.
Anywhere and everywhere I spray.
Let the blood-sucking-wretch die!
Or show up suffocating!

Befriending nooks and crannies,
To devour boys and grannies.
In automobiles or at loose ends of clothes;
It shows up for a fresh air.
What's that? Kill it! Bedbug…!!!
All panicking!
One ashamed!

I wonder if they do not outnumber us,

With their sporadic birth bus.
They bite and suck at your expense.
High, low or normal bp;
It cares not!
It wants food...blood.

Shaking my clothes in the morning,
In ferocious murmur,
And look in books for fugitives or cowards.
I hate them!
Why won't they leave us?

However, it's life's cycle;
All are dependant.
B't I hate 'em!
Leave us alone!!!

WARNING

Brian Sitta Kargbo

You are at your tricks again.
The worst has happened;
Don't do it again.

RAIN AND THE HEN

Brian Sitta Kargbo

She seeks shelter under the leaf,
I stand gazing like a hungry beef.
She is wet but stands quietly;
As the rain wets defiantly.

Her soaking gown drips down her yellow feet;
She is cold- I notice her shivering feet.
Thin hopes hang on the leaf's stalk;
She prays, "Don't let the breeze rock..."

Still in the rain,
Protected by a leaf's vein.
Gripping tight, her claws dig a well.
Ooh... she's in a cold Hell!

A star of bewilderment shines;
She's ready for a move; her face shows signs.
I thought I should help out,
Before she shrills out.

Finally, she goes bluffing;
The rain stops, sun shines, her feathers fluffing.

BEASTLY TRAVESTY
{THE VOICE OF AN ANGRY BLACK AFRICAN}

Brian Sitta Kargbo

The Rainbow Nation has lost its credence;
Mandela's fight has lost its essence;
The Zulu king stirred their conscience;
Xenophobia, this is nonsense!

Kill him! Kill her! For what?
Barbaric beings with gut!
We know of peace, but, but…?
Our tread of unity you've cut.

A repetition of history;
Inhuman act –beastly.
Ronko, and Agbada would denounce June 16
On innocent black lives you claim victory?

Your civilization is dead!
Our retribution is fed!
Mandela's face should be red!
Notoriety in foolishness his land has wed!

Religion closed its doors!
Realists were behind closed doors.
Killing Black African foreigners leaving Boors?!
South Africa has become A LAND OF BOORS!!!

ROADSIDE

Brian Sitta Kargbo

The road is not my home;
My mummy said that gnome.
Stop sluggish swag!
Run with bottle and bag!
Like a deer, run!
Zebra is not for fun!

VOICE OF THE VILLAGE

Brian Sitta Kargbo

Trapped in our hearts!
Blinded by the flashing lights of deceits!
All we get is abuse;
The existence of a hunted man.
Hunted by the past!
Hunted by the blood of the brave and innocent!
Hunted by stupidity!
Hunted by the terror of poverty and lust that sold me and me
and my people into slavery!
Left us ringing with indignation!
Twisting in uncertainty like 'Ronshow!"
Scattered us far and wide like leaves in the harmattan!

Our voices became a dormant and unused asset
After wounding our unity!
Hurting our pride!
Dislodging our hopes!
Shattered my land!
Gave us a new history;
Written on our backs! Our hands! And our heads!
Despicable men!
Alaki pipul dem!

Freedom, the light and joy of our childhood!
Becomes the tragedy of our manhood!
Bushes of laughter become bushes of despair!
Producing stench of involuntary human blood!
The air seeths revenge!
Amidst cacophonous sounds of pain!

Let the rain come and flood my mind
So I wouldn't have to think more
of the horrific moments...

I am a talking dead
With a weary heart
Yes! Under my coat is a weary heart!

Before the coming of the white man
There was so much that was good and fine!
Aaaaa we...!
But he came and wrote bold and luminous lines
Of hate and sorrow across our once joyful hearts
"Some kayn sweh mortal man!"

Ooh the white man
The white man is shallow, selfish, and insincere!
His actions are barbaric, devilish, and malign!

In this harsh world of reality
Nothing, except insanity is perfect
Ooh ya...

Our unfaltering heart hunger is freedom
FREEDOM!
We want to be free like the winds!
Slavery ought to fail! Let it fail!

FOR YOUR NOTES

Brian Sitta Kargbo (Ed.)

SIERRA LEONEAN WRITERS SERIES (SLWS)

Focusing on academic, fictional, and scientific writing that will complement other relevant materials used in schools, colleges, universities and other tertiary institutions, the Sierra Leonean Writers Series (SLWS) aims to promote good quality books by Sierra Leoneans writing on any topics and other writers from around the world who write on themes and issues about Sierra Leone.

It is the publisher's hope that students and other readers in Sierra Leone will eventually be at least some of the primary beneficiaries of these works. Not only will people in Sierra Leone be able to read materials that relate to their own lives and experiences, budding writers will also be able to draw inspiration from the efforts of their compatriots and other established writers.

Submitted work undergoes a rigorous peer-review process before being accepted for publication, with an international editorial board providing guidance to writers.

SLWS, based in Warima and Freetown in Sierra Leone, distributes books globally through AMAZON.COM. In Sierra Leone, SLWS books are currently available at the SLWS Bookshop in Warima (near Masiaka) and at CLC Bookshop, 92 Pademba Road in Freetown.

SLWS co-publishes some titles with Karantha Publishers in Sierra Leone.

For further information, please visit our website:
www.sl-writers-series.org
or contact the publisher, Prof. Osman A. Sankoh (Mallam O.)
publisher@sl-writers-series.org

Published Books – a milestone of the 50th title has been reached in September 2016!

1	Osman A. Sankoh (Mallam O.)	2001/ 2016	*A Memoir*	*Hybrid Eyes – An African in Europe*
2	Osman A. Sankoh (Mallam O.)	2001	*Non-fiction*	*Beautiful Colours*
3	Sheikh Umarr Kamarah	2002/ 2015	*Poems*	*Singing in Exile and The Child of War*
4	Abdul B. Kamara	2003/ 2015	*A Memoir*	*Unknown Destination*
5	Samuel Hinton	2003	*Poems*	*The Road to Kenema*
6	Karamoh Kabba	2005/ 2016	*A Novel*	*Morquee – The Political Drama of Wish over Wisdom*
7	Yema Lucilda Hunter	2007	*A Novel*	*Redemption Song*
8	Joe A. D. Alie	2007/ 2015	*Research Text*	*Sierra Leone Since Independence – History of a Postcolonial State*
9	Mohamed Combo Kamanda	2007	*A Play*	*The Visa*
10	J Sorie Conteh	2007	*A Novel*	*In Search of Sons*
11	Michael Fayia Kallon	2010/ 2015	*A Novel*	*The Ghosts of Ngaingah*
12	J Sorie Conteh	2011	*A Novel*	*Family Affairs*

13	Winston Forde	2011	*A Play*	*Layila, Kakatua wan bi Lida*
14	Eustace Palmer Doc P.	2012	*A Novel*	*A Pillar of the Community*
15	Siaka Kroma	2012	*Non-fiction*	*Manners Maketh Man – Adventures of a Bo School Boy*
16	Mohamed Combo Kamanda (ed)	2012	*Short Stories*	*The Price and other Short Stories from Sierra Leone*
17	Sigismond Tucker	2013	*A Memoir*	*From the Land of Diamonds to the Isle of Spice*
18	Bailah Leigh	2013	*Non-fiction*	*Dilemma of Freedom – A Diary from Behind Rebels Lines in the Sierra Leone Civil War*
19	Nnamdi Carew	2013	*A Novella*	*Tiger Fist – Two Stories*
20	Yema Lucilda Hunter	2013	*A Novel*	*Joy Came in the Morning*
21	Ebenezer 'Solo' Collier	2013	*Research Text*	*Primary & Secondary Education in Sierra Leone – Evaluation of more than 50 years of PRACTICES & POLICIES*
22	Gbananom Hallowell	2013	*Short Stories*	*Gbomgbosoro - Two Stories*
23	Sheikh Umarr Kamarah &	2013	*Poems*	**beg sol noba kuk sup** *- An Anthology*

	Majorie Jones (eds)			*of Krio Poetry*
24	Siaka Kroma	2014	*Short Stories*	*Tales from the Fireside*
25	Syl Cheney-Coker*	2014	*Poems*	*The Road to Jamaica*
26	Dr Sama Banya	2015	*A Memoir*	*Looking Back – My Life and Times*
27	Andrew K Keili	2015	*Social Commentary*	*Ponder My Thoughts – Vol. 1*
28	Jedidah A. O. Johnson	2015	*A Novel*	*Youthful Yearnings*
29	Oumar Farouk Sesay	2015	*A Novel*	*Landscape of Memories*
30	Oumar Farouk Sesay	2015	*Poems*	*The Edge of a Cry*
31	Gbanabom Hallowell	2015	*A Novel*	*The Road to Kaibara*
32	Mohamed Gibril Sesay*	2015	*A Novel*	*This Side of Nothingness*
33	Yema Lucilda Hunter	2015	*A Novel*	*Nanna*
34	Yusuf Bangura	2015	*Research Text*	*Development, Democracy & Cohesion*
35	Lansana Gberie	2015	*Research Text*	*War, Politics & Justice in West Africa*
36	Yema Lucilda Hunter	2015	*A Biography*	*An African Treasure: In Search of Gladys Casely-Hayford 1904-1950*
37	Moses Kainwo	2015	*Poems*	*Ayo Ayo Ayo and other Love Songs*

38	Abdulai Walon-Jalloh	2015	*Poems*	*Voices and Passions*
39	Gbanabom Hallowell (Ed.)	2016	*Short Stories*	*In the Belly of the Lion – An Anthology of new Sierra Leonean Short Stories*
40	Ahmed Koroma	2016	*Poems*	*Along the Odokoko River - Poems*
41	George Coleridge-Taylor	2016	*A Memoir*	*Transformation in Transition*
42	Karamoh Kabba	2016	*Research Text*	*Fire from Timbuktu: A Dialogue with History*
43	Umu Kultumie Tejan-Jalloh	2016	*A Memoir*	*Telling It As It Was: The Career of A Sierra Leonean Woman in Public Service*
44	Ambrose Massaquoi	2016	*Poems*	*Along the Peal of Drums: Collected Poems (1990-2015)*
45	Mohamed Gibril Sesay	2016	*Poems*	*At the Gathering of Roads (Poems)*
46	Gbanabom Hallowell	2016	*Poems*	*Manscape in the Sierra: New and Collected Poems 1991-2011*
47	Gbanabom Hallowell (Ed.)	2016	*Short Stories and Poems*	*Leoneanthology: Comtemporary Short Stories and Poems from Sierra Leone*
48	Gbanabom Hallowell	2016	*Poems*	*Don't Call Me Elvis and Other Poems*

| 49 | Bakar Mansaray | 2016 | *Short Stories* | *A Suitcase Full of Dried Fish and Other Stories* |
| 50 | Gbanabom Hallowell | 2016 | *Poems* | *The Art of the Lonely Wanderer* |

*co-published with Karantha Publishers